MARGRET & H.A

You Can Do It, Curious George!

HOUGHTON MIFFLIN HARCOURT

School Publishers

Acknowledgments

Curious George by Margret and H.A. Rey by Catherine Hapka. Copyright © 2008 Houghton Mifflin Harcourt Publishing Company. All rights reserved. The character Curious George®, including without limitation the character's name and the character's likenesses, are registered trademarks of Houghton Mifflin Harcourt Publishing Company. Curious George logo is a trademark of Houghton Mifflin Harcourt Publishing Company.

"Whistling" from *Rainy Rainy Saturday* by Jack Prelutsky. Copyright © 1980 by Jack Prelutsky. Reprinted by permission of HarperCollins Publishers.

"Time to Play" by Nikki Grimes. Copyright © 1991 by Nikki Grimes. Reprinted by permission of Curtis Brown, Ltd.

"By Myself," from *Honey, I Love* by Eloise Greenfield. Text copyright © 1972 by Eloise Greenfield. Reprinted by permission of HarperCollins Publishers.

Credits

Illustration

26–27 Mike Reed; 28–29 Steve Cox; 30 Don Tate.

Printed in China

Little Big Book ISBN: 978-0-547-88487-5
Big Book ISBN: 978-0-547-88479-0

9 10 11 12 13 14   0940   21 20 19 18 17 16

4500573885   A B C D E F G

Table of Contents

Paired Selections

This is George.

He was a good little monkey and always very curious.

George loved going to the museum with his friend.

While they were visiting the museum, they saw a sign.

The sign said that the museum had won a prize.

People voted this museum as their favorite.

They said this museum was the BEST!

When George saw the sign, he started to think.

What could he do best?

He decided to find out.

"You can do it, George!" said the man with
the yellow hat.

George went back home.

He was good at drawing dinosaurs.

Maybe he could draw the best dinosaur picture ever!

George decided that he liked to draw, but he
wanted to try to do something different!
He climbed out the window to look for ideas.

Soon George came to a restaurant.

That gave him a great idea!

George loved spaghetti.

He decided he would make the best spaghetti ever.

You can do it, George!

Look at all that spaghetti!
George thought it tasted great.
He tasted more and more of it—
and made a big mess.

Then the chef came in.

"Get out!" he shouted.

"Out of my kitchen!"

George was going to have to find

something else he did best.

George needed another idea.

He got on a bus to think.

The bus took him to the ski slope.

That gave George an idea.

He grabbed the biggest sled he could find.

Maybe he could sled down the hill faster
than anyone ever had before.

You can do it, George!

At first sledding was fun.

Then George started going too fast.

Look out, George!
George was going to have to find
something else he did best.

George needed another idea.

Then he remembered something he did
better than anyone.

He rushed back home.

When he got there he took out his kite.
He was going to be the best kite flyer ever!

17

George got his kite to go higher and higher.

You can do it, George!

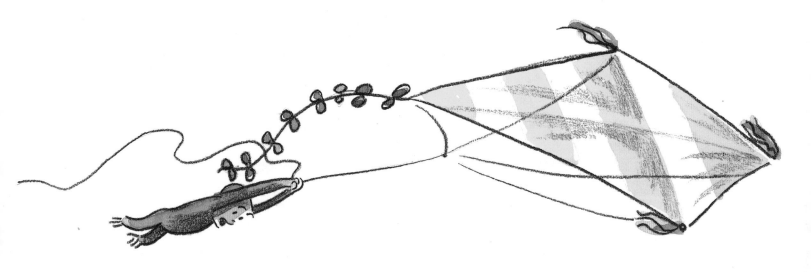

Then the kite lifted George right off
the ground!
Look out below!

George landed in a tree in the forest.

His kite flew away without him.

George was going to have to find

something else he did best.

Just then
George spotted smoke.
Oh, no!
It was a forest fire!

George wanted to warn everybody about the fire.

He raced to town and found the fire station.

The fire fighters quickly put out the fire.

Whew!

By now the sun was setting.

It was too late for George to figure out
what he did best.

George's friend met him back at the museum.

The director had heard that George warned everyone about the forest fire.

She thought that was the BEST thing anyone had done in a long time.

George did it! Hooray!

He found out what he can do best.

He is the Best Helper.

George got a very special prize that day!

Whistling

by Jack Prelutsky

Oh, I can laugh and I can sing
and I can scream and shout,
but when I try to whistle,
the whistle won't come out.

I shape my lips the proper way,
I make them small and round,
but when I blow, just air comes out,
there is no whistling sound.

But I'll keep trying very hard
to whistle loud and clear,
and someday soon I'll whistle tunes
for everyone to hear.

Time to Play

by Nikki Grimes

Mama says to play outside.

Wish I had a bike to ride.

I'll fly to the moon instead.

Steer the rocket in my head.

I'll pretend to find a star

no one else has seen so far.

Then I'll name it after me —

Africa Lawanda Lee!

But for now I'll grab some chalk,

play hopscotch out on the walk.

By Myself

by Eloise Greenfield

When I'm by myself

And I close my eyes

I'm a twin

I'm a dimple in a chin

I'm a room full of toys

I'm a squeaky noise

I'm a gospel song

I'm a gong

I'm a leaf turning red

I'm a loaf of brown bread

I'm a whatever I want to be

An anything I care to be

And when I open my eyes

What I care to be

Is me